# IT'S TIME TO EAT SOUP

# It's Time to Eat SOUP

Walter the Educator

Silent King Books
A WhichHead Entertainment Imprint

Copyright © 2024 by Walter the Educator

All rights reserved. No part of this book may be reproduced in any manner whatsoever without written per- mission except in the case of brief quotations embodied in critical articles and reviews.

First Printing, 2024

Disclaimer

This book is a literary work; the story is not about specific persons, locations, situations, and/or circumstances unless mentioned in a historical context. Any resemblance to real persons, locations, situations, and/or circumstances is coincidental. This book is for entertainment and informational purposes only. The author and publisher offer this information without warranties expressed or implied. No matter the grounds, neither the author nor the publisher will be accountable for any losses, injuries, or other damages caused by the reader's use of this book. The use of this book acknowledges an understanding and acceptance of this disclaimer.

It's Time to Eat SOUP is a collectible early learning book by Walter the Educator suitable for all ages belonging to Walter the Educator's Time to Eat Book Series. Collect more books at WaltertheEducator.com

**USE THE EXTRA SPACE TO TAKE NOTES AND DOCUMENT YOUR MEMORIES**

# SOUP

It's time to eat soup, so warm and so nice,

# It's Time to Eat

# Soup

A bowl full of comfort, like hugs in a slice.

It's steamy and tasty, so cozy and neat,

Soup is the best when you're ready to eat!

Tomato soup's red, so smooth and so sweet,

Dip in your sandwich, it's the perfect treat.

Chicken noodle's yummy, with broth so clear,

Each spoonful's a treasure to bring you good cheer!

Carrots and celery float in the pot,

With noodles or rice, soup hits the spot!

Add beans or potatoes, whatever you choose,

There's no wrong in soup, you'll never lose!

Pumpkin soup's creamy, so orange and bright,

It's perfect for dinner on a chilly night.

Or try some minestrone, with veggies galore,

Every bowl is a journey to explore!

## It's Time to Eat

# Soup

Slurp it with spoons, or sip it real slow,

Soup warms you up when it's cold and there's snow.

With each hearty bite, you'll feel so snug,

Soup's like a blanket, a big, cozy hug.

Broccoli cheddar is cheesy and green,

It's one of the best soups you've ever seen.

Or try some tortilla, with spice and zest,

Every bowl's different, but all are the best!

Soup can be chunky or smooth as a dream,

With meat, tofu, or veggies, it's always supreme.

It's cooked in a pot, where flavors combine,

Soup's like a party in one tasty line!

Making soup's fun, stir the pot with care,

Add all your favorites, there's plenty to share.

Invite your family, your friends, or your pup,

## It's Time to Eat

# Soup

Soup tastes even better when you all team up!

When your tummy's grumbling, there's one thing to do,

Heat up some soup, it's ready for you!

A bowl of pure magic, so warm and deep,

Soup is the meal you'll always keep!

So let's cheer for soup, the meal we adore,

With flavors and love, it gives us much more.

Say it out loud, let's all give a whoop,

# It's Time to Eat

# Soup

"Hooray for the joy of delicious soup!"

# ABOUT THE CREATOR

Walter the Educator is one of the pseudonyms for Walter Anderson. Formally educated in Chemistry, Business, and Education, he is an educator, an author, a diverse entrepreneur, and he is the son of a disabled war veteran. "Walter the Educator" shares his time between educating and creating. He holds interests and owns several creative projects that entertain, enlighten, enhance, and educate, hoping to inspire and motivate you. Follow, find new works, and stay up to date with Walter the Educator™

**at WaltertheEducator.com**

www.ingramcontent.com/pod-product-compliance
Lightning Source LLC
LaVergne TN
LVHW052015060526
838201LV00059B/4039